DESERTS AROUND THE WORLD

The Great Victoria Desert

By Lynn Peppas

Crabtree Publishing Company
www.crabtreebooks.com

Crabtree Publishing Company

www.crabtreebooks.com

Author: Lynn Peppas
Publishing plan research and development:
Sean Charlebois, Reagan Miller
Crabtree Publishing Company
Editor and indexer: Wendy Scavuzzo
Design and photo research: Katherine Berti
Project coordinator: Kathy Middleton
Print and production coordinator: Katherine Berti

Picture credits:
© Jean-Marc La Roque/AUSCAPE: page 16
© DWSP/S.Sadler: pages 4, 9
Shutterstock: cover, pages 1, 5 (Kalgoorlie), 7, 8, 10, 12, 13 (right), 14, 15, 21, 22, 23 (Super Pit), 25, 26 (background), 28 (bottom); fritz16: page 17
Thinkstock: pages 5 (top), 6, 13 (left), 24, 28 (top)
Wikimedia Commons: Dr. Martin Schmieder, Perth: page 5 (Lake Acraman); Heiko Volland: page 5 (Nullarbor Plain); Gazjo: page 5 (Gibson Desert): Joe Weber: page 11; Sj199998: page 18; Sean Mack: page 19 (top); National Library of Australia: page 19 (bottom); Chris Winerflood: page 20; Lodo27: page 21 (top); Rob Lavinsky: page 23 (gold); Wayne England: page 26 (inset)

Library and Archives Canada Cataloguing in Publication

Peppas, Lynn
The Great Victoria Desert / Lynn Peppas.

(Deserts around the world)
Includes index.
Issued also in electronic formats.
ISBN 978-0-7787-0711-0 (bound).--ISBN 978-0-7787-0719-6 (pbk.)

1. Great Victoria Desert (S. Aust. and W.A.)--Juvenile literature. I. Title. II. Series: Deserts around the world (St. Catharines, Ont.)

DU380.G74P46 2012 j994.1'5 C2012-905684-7

Library of Congress Cataloging-in-Publication Data

CIP available at Library of Congress

Crabtree Publishing Company

www.crabtreebooks.com 1-800-387-7650

Printed in Canada/102012/MA20120817

Published in Canada
Crabtree Publishing
616 Welland Ave.
St. Catharines, Ontario
L2M 5V6

Published in the United States
Crabtree Publishing
PMB 59051
350 Fifth Avenue, 59th Floor
New York, New York 10118

Published in the United Kingdom
Crabtree Publishing
Maritime House
Basin Road North, Hove
BN41 1WR

Published in Australia
Crabtree Publishing
3 Charles Street
Coburg North
VIC 3058

CONTENTS

Words that are defined in the glossary are in **bold** type the first time they appear in the text.

CHAPTER 1

The Great Victoria Desert

The Great Victoria Desert is the largest desert in Australia. It has an area of about 161,700 square miles (418,800 sq km). It is the least populated area in Australia. It is a hot, arid desert located in central Australia. Arid areas of the desert usually receive about 8–10 inches (20–25 cm) of rainfall annually.

FAST FACT

Australia came by its name from the Latin word, *Australis*, which means "southern," and was named for its southern locale. It is also sometimes referred to by the term "down under" because, when viewing it on a map of the world, it is one of the lowest countries in the southern hemisphere.

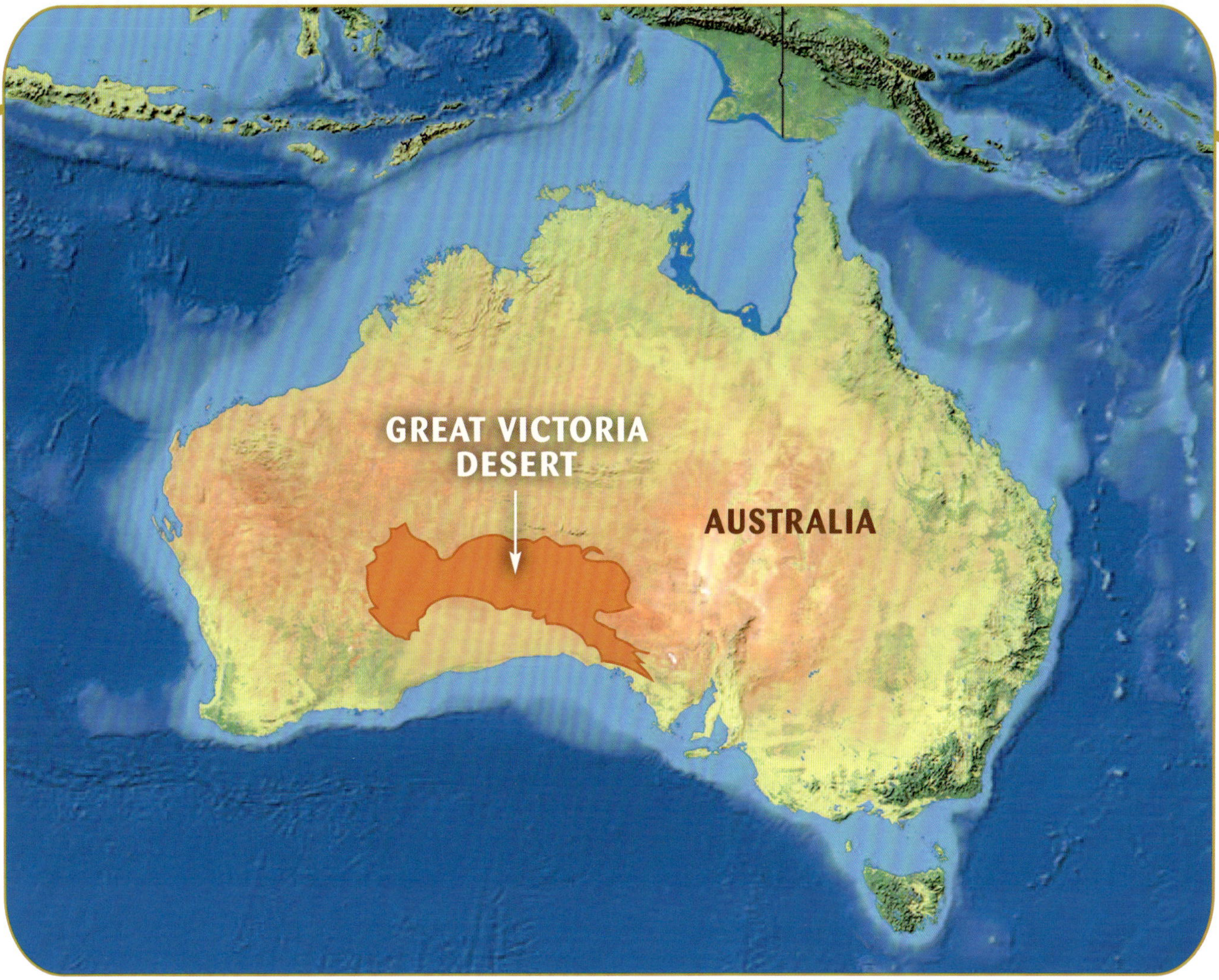

GREAT VICTORIA DESERT

AUSTRALIA

Location of the Great Victoria Desert

The Great Victoria Desert stretches between the two Australian states of Western Australia and South Australia. Its eastern border is along the Eastern Goldfields, near the cities of Kalgoorlie and Laverton in the state of Western Australia. It extends westward to the Stuart and Gawler Ranges. To the south of the desert lies the Nullarbor Plain, and in the northernmost regions, the Little Sandy Desert, and the Gibson Desert make up part of the northern border.

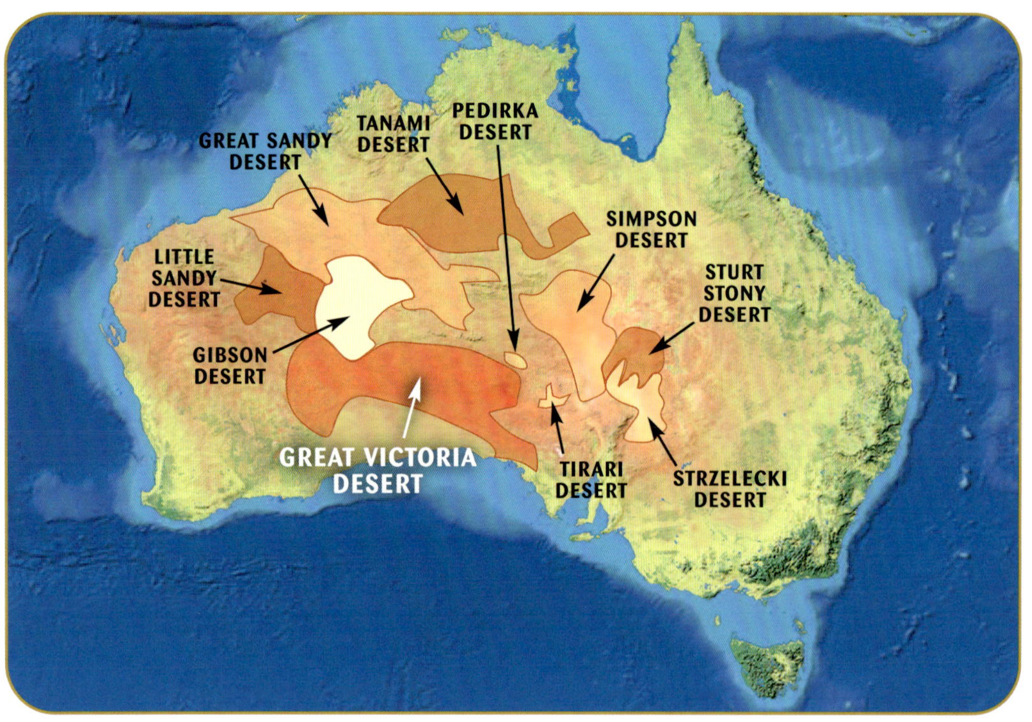

Outback is a term that Australians use to describe the rugged, unsettled, desert-like areas found in central Australia. The Great Victoria Desert is one of ten deserts included in the Australian Outback.

Australia: The Land Down Under

Australia is both the name of a country and continent. Australia, the continent, consists of the mainland of Australia and the island of Tasmania. Australia is also the driest inhabited continent on Earth.

Australia, the country, is officially known as the Commonwealth of Australia. It has six states and is home to over 22 million people of many different cultures. Sydney is the largest city in Australia and more than 4.5 million people live there. From here on, any mention of Australia will be referring only to the mainland country.

Demographics of Australia

The majority of Australians live in coastal areas on the mainland. Central Australia is home to ten deserts: Great Victoria, Great Sandy, Tanami, Simpson, Gibson, Little Sandy, Strzelecki, Sturt Stony, Tirari, and Pedirka. These deserts make up almost 20 percent of the area of mainland Australia.

Salt Lake Sculptures

Lake Ballard is a salt lake found near Menzies, Australia, on the western side of the GVD. In 2003, British sculptor Antony Gormley installed on Lake Ballard an outdoor exhibition of 51 life-sized sculptures of human figures called *Inside Australia*. People who want to view the exhibition are warned to take plenty of water with them and to not travel alone because of the dangerous desert conditions.

Artist Antony Gormley's sculptures of human figures are scattered over an area of 4 square miles (10 sq km) on the salt lake Lake Ballard. Gormley based his designs on laser scans of people who lived in the nearby town of Menzies, Australia.

NOTABLE QUOTE

"Geographical features have been terribly scarce upon this expedition, and this peculiar spring is the first permanent water I have found. I have ventured to dedicate it to our most gracious Queen. The great desert in which I found it, and which will most probably extend to the west as far as it does to the east, I have also honoured with Her Majesty's mighty name, calling it the Great Victoria Desert, and the spring, Queen Victoria's Spring."

—Ernest Giles from *Australia twice traversed*, journals written from 1872–1876

CHAPTER 2

The Unique Geography of the GVD

The Great Victoria Desert is an area with grassland plains, gibber plains, salt lakes, and red sand dunes. Much of the GVD is covered with open woodlands of eucalyptus trees, and grasses called **spinifex**. It is home to a unique variety of plants and animals that are not naturally found in any other country on Earth.

Spinifex grasses grow in spiky clumps across vast stretches of the GVD. They are an important part of the ecosystem because they prevent the sand from blowing away.

Red-colored sands—found primarily in the GVD—may contain clay, or be surrounded by **iron oxide**. It takes thousands of years for sand to be coated with iron oxide.

Sand Dunes

The Great Victoria Desert has the longest, and some of the largest sand dunes of all the hot deserts on Earth. Sand dunes are a common image that is often associated with deserts but, in reality, sand dunes cover only about 15 percent of Earth's deserts. The Great Victoria Desert leads other deserts, in that it is almost covered in red sand dunes. These great dunes run in an east-west direction and are about 65 feet (20 m) high and some are over 330 feet (100 m) long.

Gibber Plains

Gibber plains are areas where the soil is covered by a closely packed layer of small pebblesand small angular rocks that are covered with a thin layer of iron oxide. They are sometimes called desert pavement because that is what it looks like. Gibber plains do not usually support vegetation, except for during periods of heavy rains when flowering plants cover the areas.

Gibber plains are a common site in the GVD and support very little vegetation during dry spells.

Salt Lakes

Salt lakes are also called playas or salt pans. Many salt lakes located in the Great Victoria Desert are a result of palaeodrainage basins, which are ancient, freshwater lakes that dried up long ago. There are many salt lakes throughout the GVD. One of the largest is Lake Ballard near Menzies, Australia. The Serpentine Lakes in the Great Victoria Desert are salt lakes located near the Mamungari Conservation Park, which is near the border between Western Australia and South Australia.

Geology of the Great Victoria Desert

The Great Victoria Desert is home to some of the oldest rocks on Earth. On the western side of the desert, the underlying ancient Yilgarn **Craton** contains rocks estimated to be about 2.5 billion years old. To the north of the desert, the Musgrave Block contains rocks more than 1 billion years old. The Gawler Craton, estimated to be about 2 billion years old, exists underneath the eastern part of the desert. The Officer Basin is located between the states of Western Australia and South Australia. The basin is a very hard layer or shield of rock on which younger sedimentary rock has formed over millions of years. The Officer Creek drains a portion of the basin.

Rock from the Yilgarn Craton is some of the oldest found on Earth.

Subtropical Desert

The GVD is a subtropical desert. The desert is located between two prevailing wind belts that run in a north-south direction.

Climate of the Great Victoria Desert

The GVD is classified as a hot desert. Hot desert climates experience exceptionally hot periods throughout the year. In the summer months, the desert reaches temperatures that range from 86–104°F (30–40°C) in the daytime. In the winter months, the temperature averages between 60–75°F (16–24°C). Evenings in the desert are much cooler. Nighttime temperatures range from around 66°F (19°C) during the summer months to freezing temperatures during the winter.

The Great Victoria Desert is an arid desert that receives unpredictable rainfall. The desert receives between 8–10 inches (20–25 cm) of rain per year. The northern areas of the desert receive less rain than the more southern areas.

FAST FACT

In the southern hemisphere, seasons occur at opposite times of the year than in the northern hemisphere. In countries such as Australia, summer is from December to February and winter is from June to August.

Wildlife in the Great Victoria Desert

Even though the GVD has an arid climate, many animals have special adaptations that make it possible for them to live in this challenging terrain. For the most part, the area is unpopulated by humans. This allows wildlife populations to flourish without concern of losing their habitat.

Sand Goanna

Lizards

The Great Victoria Desert is known for its variety of lizard species. One such lizard is the great desert skink. It was once thought to be extinct, but was rediscovered living in the Great Victoria Desert in 1998. The great desert skink has copper-colored scales and grows to be about 7 inches (18 cm) long. They build and live in burrows that allow them to stay cool during hot daytime hours, and stay warm during cold nights. Their burrows can be up to 40 feet (12 m) long. A much larger lizard living in the GVD is the sand goanna. It has a forked tongue, similar to that of a snake. It is a **diurnal** animal, which means it is mostly active during daylight hours. The sand goanna can grow to about 4.5 feet (137 cm) long and can weigh up to 13 pounds (6 kg). They eat small rodents, large insects, and smaller lizards. This much larger lizard digs an underground burrows, too.

Dingoes

The dingo is a medium-sized wild dog that has lived in Australia for over 3,000 years. They grow to be about 3 feet (1 m) long. The dingo has tan to black fur, large ears, a keen sense of smell, and excellent eyesight. They often hunt at night in packs although they also hunt alone. They eat rats, kangaroos, rabbits, and farm animals such as sheep.

Malleefowl

The Malleefowl is a type of bird that lives in the Australian desert areas such as the GVD. They live on the ground and somewhat resemble a **domestic** chicken. They can only fly very short distances to escape danger or reach a branch of a tree. Malleefowl parent birds scratch out a mound of sand about 10–16 feet (3–5 m) in diameter and more than 3 feet (1 m) high. They fill it up with twigs, leaves, and other natural materials to create a kind of compost. They dig an egg chamber in the composted material in which the female lays up to 25 eggs. The birds then completely cover the compost and eggs in a thick layer of sand. The composted material rots and produces a heat that **incubates** the eggs. When the chicks hatch, they must work their way out of the compost-covered egg chamber. This takes them about half a day. The baby birds take cover in nearby mallee shrubs for protection from predators.

Red Kangaroos

Kangaroos are native to the continent of Australia. The Red Kangaroo is the largest **marsupial** on Earth. They have long hind feet and powerful hind legs that allow them to jump lengths of up to 30 feet (9 m). Traveling by jumping allows kangaroos to conserve energy. A full-grown red kangaroo can be up to 5 feet (1.5 m) tall and weigh up to 300 pounds (136 kg). Red kangaroos are **nocturnal**, and have adapted to the hot climate by remaining inactive during the hot daytime hours. They also have an insulating layer of fur. They are herbivores and they conserve water from the vegetation they eat. Their kidneys help them survive in the dry climate by concentrating urine to help them conserve water.

Invasive Species Living in the GVD

Invasive species are animals that are not native to an area and, as a result, cause destruction to the environment and other native species of animals. Invasive animals living in the GVD include rabbits, camels, and **feral** cats and goats. These animals compete with other native animals for sources of food and water in the desert. This has led to the extinction of native GVD animals such as the lesser bilby and the desert bandicoot.

Plant Life in the GVD

Large areas of the GVD are open woodlands, which are areas with scattered trees whose canopies cover less than 30 percent of the ground. Large stretches of grassland plains are covered with desert grasses called spinifex.

Spinifex

Spinifex is a long, spiky type of grass that grows throughout much of the GVD. This very hardy desert plant grows in dense clumps on sandy or rocky soils. An adaptation that helps the plant survive during dry spells is its ability to roll its leaves into cylinders so they do not lose water through evaporation.

Acacias

Acacias in Australia are commonly called "wattle." Acacias are a fast-growing, prickly shrub or tall tree that grows in the Australian deserts, and in several other hot, dry places in the world. After heavy rainfall, these plants produce furry, round, yellow blooms. Mulga is a type of Acacia that grows in the GVD. At maturity, it can reach a height of 32 feet (10 m). It has an umbrella-shaped canopy of narrow, gray leaves. These leaves are very tough and do not lose water easily. The large canopy directs any rainwater toward the tree's trunk and downward to the roots.

Eucalyptus

Many different kinds of eucalyptus trees grow throughout the GVD. Sometimes they are called gum trees because they ooze a sticky sap when the bark of the tree is broken. A eucalyptus tree grows a single trunk. But if the tree is burned in a brush fire, it grows back as a group of multiple, thin-stemmed trees called a mallee. Mallee trees can also grow from a lignotuber root. A lignotuber root grows underground and sends multiple stems upward when the original tree is damaged by fire. Many eucalyptus trees flower after heavy rainfall.

The marble gum tree is one of the tallest trees in the GVD. It is a species of eucalyptus that grows to a height of up to 66 feet (20 m).

NOTABLE QUOTE

"...we immediately entered dense scrubs, composed as usual of mallee, with its friend the spinifex, black oaks, and numerous gigantic mallee-like gum-trees."

—Explorer Ernest Giles talks of the GVD in his memoir *Australia twice traversed.*

CHAPTER 3

Living in the Great Victoria Desert

The GVD is home to numerous conservation reserves, and Aboriginal lands such as the Aṉangu Pitjantjatjara and Maralinga Tjarutja lands. National parks include the Great Victoria Desert Nature Reserve, Yeo Lake Nature Reserve, Neale Junction Nature Reserve, Tallaringa Conservation Park, Yellabinna Regional Reserve, Yumbarra Conservation Park, and the Mamungari Conservation Park. Much of the area is sparsely inhabited. Highways in the area are actually dirt roads that are difficult to travel on without specialized four-wheel-drive vehicles.

Highways that cross GVD reserves do not resemble paved highways such as those in North America. They are simply dirt roads or paths like the highway below in the Maralinga Tjarutja lands.

Aboriginal Peoples

Several tribes of **aboriginal** peoples have lived in Australia for over 40,000 years. Those living inland moved to the desert areas over 20,000 years ago. Thousands of years ago, **Aborigines** were **nomadic** hunter-gatherers who depended on their natural environment for survival.

Aborigines living in desert areas moved from one water source to the next in small family groups. Knowledge of these areas of water and food sources was passed down through generations. Aborigines who lived in the desert areas adapted to the dry conditions by allowing other tribes to hunt in their territories during dry spells. They also dug up black oak tree roots for a source of water.

Nomadic Aborigines protected themselves with shelters called windbreaks, which were tree limbs covered with bark or brush. Aborigines traveled with fire sticks with which to start small fires to keep them warm during cold desert nights. They often traveled with domesticated dingoes that also which provided warmth during cold evenings.

There are multiple groups of Aborigines living in the Great Victoria Desert such as the Pitjantjatjara, Ngaanyatjarra, and Yankunytjatjara peoples. Aborigines who speak different dialects of the Western Desert language are called Aṉangu Aborigines. Aṉangu means "human being" in the Western Desert language, but today it refers to the Aborigines who live in the desert area. The Pila Nguru are sometimes called the Spinifex people because they live in an area of spinifex grasses. Their name means "home country in the flat between sandhills." They live in the state of Western Australia in the Great Victoria Desert just north of the Nullarbor Plain.

Musically talented Aborigines have played a wind instrument called the didgeridoo for over 1,000 years throughout Australia.

Tjukurpa

Tjukurpa is the spiritual beliefs, cultural traditions, and social rules that Australian Aborigines live by. It explains the creation of the world, daily existence, and the relationship between all living things. Australian Aborigines believe that it is their responsibility to maintain the natural balance of the plants and animals living in areas such as the Great Victoria Desert. Tjukurpa is knowledge passed down from generation to generation that teaches the Aṉangu people how to take care of all living things and the land. It also passes down the locations of important water sources that are otherwise unknown.

British Colonization of Australia

The British colonized Australia and claimed parts of the continent as British lands in the late 1700s. British settlers brought diseases such as chickenpox, smallpox, influenza, and measles, which the Australian aboriginal peoples had no against, and many died as a result. Many were mistreated by British settlers and used for slave labor. Aborigines were not allowed to vote in Australian federal government elections until 1962.

Indigenous Protected Areas

Many large areas of the GVD have been designated as belonging to the **indigenous** peoples. In 1981, the Australian government granted land rights to the Aṉangu peoples in South Australia with the Aṉangu Pitjantjatjara Yankunytjatjara Land Rights Act of 1981. This act meant that the aboriginal peoples living in the Great Victoria Desert had total rights over large areas of the desert's land. In fact, travelers in the area must apply for special permits to cross these aboriginal-owned lands.

Watarru

Watarru is an indigenous protected area in the Great Victoria Desert with an area of over 4,600 square miles (11,914 sq km). It is located near the northwestern border in the state of South Australia. The Aṉangu Aborigines manage the land according to their culture and traditional laws that have been passed down for thousands of years.

The Watarru Aṉangu Community has a population of about 60 people.

Sources of Water in the GVD

Freshwater Pipeline

The Goldfields Water Supply pipeline began delivering water to gold prospectors and miners in the early 1900s. The pipeline is still in operation today, and supplies water to farms, mines, and over 100,000 people living in the western area of the GVD.

Goldfields Water Supply pipeline

Artesian Bore

The town of Coober Pedy is supplied with water from 197-foot (60 m) deep **artesian bores** drilled in the area. The water can be purchased for about 20 cents for 8 gallons (30 L).

Ooldea Soak

The Ooldea Soak is an important and permanent freshwater source found on the southern border of the GVD. It has been a water source and trading center for many different tribes of Aborigines for thousands of years. It is found within a large, sandy depression surrounded by high, red sand dunes.

A European woman named Daisy Bates moved to the Ooldea area in 1919 and began a mission that provided food and medical care for Aborigine peoples.

NOTABLE QUOTE

"Ooldea water is one of Nature's miracles in barren Central Australia...Even in the cruelest droughts it had never failed. Here the tribes gathered in their hundreds for initiation and other ceremonies. When all the waters had dried for countless miles came strangers from afar offering their flints and their food...for the right to share it and live."

—from the article "My Natives And I: Life Story Of Daisy M. Bates" in *The Advertiser*, Adelaide, SA, Feb. 6, 1936.

Mamungari Conservation Park

The Mamungari Conservation Park was called the Unnamed Conservation Park for over 35 years. It was given its current name in November 2006. The Aṉangu peoples settled in the area about 39,000 years ago and now manage the land. Mamungari Conservation Park has an area of about 8,100 square miles (21,000 sq km). The park has changed very little over time and is known as one of the most remote conservation areas on Earth. It was listed as a Biosphere Reserve under UNESCO Man and Biosphere Program in 1977. The program works toward improving the relationship between people and their environment.

Ernest Giles—Great Victoria Desert's First European Explorer

Ernest Giles moved to Australia from England in 1851. He began exploring central Australia in 1872. Giles was the first European explorer to cross overland from South to Western Australia in 1875. He discovered the Great Victoria Springs, and named the Great Victoria Desert after the queen of Great Britain at the time, Queen Victoria. Giles published books on his expeditions and advanced knowledge about Australian deserts such as the GVD. During his lifetime, he was awarded a gold medal from the Royal Geographical Society in London, England, and a knighthood from Italy.

Len Beadell

Len Beadell was a surveyor with the Australian Army. In 1947, the governments of Australia and Britain asked him to find a place in Australia to create a rocket-testing range. He chose the Woomera area in the GVD. Beadell also created over 4,039 miles (6,500 km) of new roads to move scientists and other army personal throughout the GVD and other desert areas. These roads opened up much of the Great Victoria Desert. Mount Beadell was named after the desert explorer by the Surveyor General of Western Australia in 1958. Beadell received numerous awards for his surveying work including the British Empire Medal in 1958 for the construction of the Gunbarrel Highway, and the Order of Australia in 1988. A memorial was also built at the top of Mount Beadell a year after his death.

An original marker plate from Len Beadell remains in the GVD at an intersection of two highways.

Living underground means that no heating or air conditioning units are needed. The temperature inside the dugout remains at around a comfortable 73–77°F (23–25°C) all year round.

Dugout Dwellings at Coober Pedy

Coober Pedy is a small town located on the Stuart Highway in the eastern border of the Great Victoria Desert. It has a population of about 3,500 people. It is Australia's oldest and largest opal mining town. To escape the extreme temperatures of the desert, some of the town's inhabitants live in underground homes called dugouts. These underground homes have rooms such as bedrooms, living rooms, and kitchens much like regular residences. They are not deep caves but instead dug out of hillsides of sandstone—a strong type of rock that adds stability to the home. Doorways sit at street level. Underground rooms are ventilated with narrow, vertical shafts that rise to, and stick out of, the surface of hillsides.

Dingo Fence

The Dingo Fence—also called the Dog Fence or Great Barrier Fence—is 3,488 miles (5,614 km) long. It runs from Surfers Paradise in Queensland to the Bight near Western Australia. Built from 1880–1885, it is one of the longest fences in the world. It was built to keep dingoes from killing sheep in Queensland, Australia.

Dingo Fence

CHAPTER 4

Trade and Commerce

Many people living in the GVD do so for employment reasons. Residents work in mines, tourism, or are army personnel working on space programs and defense systems.

The town of Coober Pedy, shown here, has a population of about 3,500 people. Most work in the opal mines or the tourism industry.

Opal Mining

Coober Pedy, located on the eastern border of the GVD, is the largest opal mining area in the world. About 70 percent of Earth's opals are mined from the area. Opals were first found at Coober Pedy in February 1915 by a 14-year-old boy named Willie Hutchison. Hutchison was part of a gold prospecting party and had been looking for water in the Coober Pedy area. He returned to camp after finding water and half a bag of opal.

FAST FACT

The world's largest uncut opal was found at Coober Pedy. It weighed 7.7 pounds (3.5 kg). It was named Olympic Australis because it was found in 1956—the year that the Olympic Games were held in Australia.

Gold Mining in the Great Victoria Desert

Gold was first discovered in Australia near the western border of the Great Victoria Desert in 1893 by gold prospectors, Paddy Hannan, Tom Flanagan, and Daniel Shea. A gold rush in the area, called Kalgoorlie today, followed shortly after. Since the three prospectors' original 1893 claim, many large gold mines have been dug nearby. The area is called "the Golden Mile" and is considered to be one of the richest gold deposits ever discovered. The discovery opened the area up, along with the development of railways to transport goods and resources to and from the area.

The Super Pit

The Super Pit was Australia's largest open-pit gold mine up to 2012. It is located in Kalgoorlie, Western Australia. When finished, the Super Pit will be 2.4 miles (3.8 km) long, 1 mile (1.5 km) wide, and 1,959 feet (600 m) deep. It produces up to 850,000 ounces (24 metric tonnes) of gold every year. Gold was discovered in 2005 at the proposed Tropicana Mine. Since then, a mining company has begun an open-pit mine to be ready by 2013. The open-pit area is estimated to be 3.1 miles (5 km) long, 0.7 miles (1.2 km) wide, and 3,281 feet (1,000 m) deep.

The Super Pit

Oil and Gas Exploration

Naturally occurring basins, such as the Officer Basin in the Great Victoria Desert, are believed to be prime areas for oil discoveries. Several oil and gas companies started exploring the area in the 1960s. Exploration is still continued today in most areas, except for in the Mamungari Conservation Park. Australia has more than 50 basins, 12 of which are producing oil and gas.

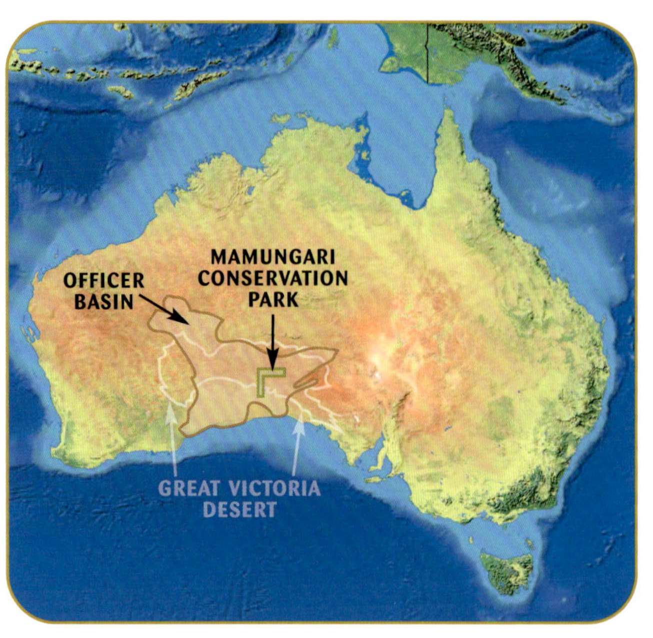

Rocket Launch Site at Woomera

Woomera Prohibited Area is the site of a rocket-testing range that was first established by the British and Australian governments in 1947. The area was used to experiment with and launch rockets and missiles. The location was also used by the United States for the Deep Space Station 41 project from the mid-50s to the mid-70s. In 1969, the Australian Department of Defence and the United States Air Force created the Nurrungar Joint Tracking Facility a few miles from Woomera. For 30 years, this facility provided early detection of nuclear missile launches from a space-based surveillance. It is no longer in operation. Most of the Woomera Prohibited Area is off-limits to the public today. The Royal Australian Air Force (RAAF) now uses the land as a military testing site for defense systems.

Tourism at Woomera

Woomera is a small town in the GVD, located on the southeast corner of the Woomera Prohibited Area. The town was opened to the public in 1982. Within the town of Woomera, tourists can visit different attractions. The Woomera National Aerospace and Missile Park showcases missiles, rockets, and aircraft which were tested in the area for the past 60 years. The Woomera Rocket Range Museum houses historical displays about the Woomera Range and its founder, Len Beadell.

The Woomera Rocket Park is a popular tourist attraction in Woomera. The park features rocket shells and aircraft that have been tested there over the past 50 years.

NOTABLE QUOTE

"For a town of 300 in outback Australia… We have tenpin bowling, squash courts, a pool, cinema, large hotel and a gymnasium better equipped than you'll find in Sydney [Australia]."

—Garry Clarke, Manager of Corporate Services and Infrastructure at Woomera (2006) from "Australian Geographic"

CHAPTER 5

Desert at Risk

The GVD has had to overcome a number of challenges over the past 50 years that has put the desert at risk. Military weapons, along with environmental processes such as desertification, have taken its toll on the health of the desert and its residents. National and international organizations are working to clean up and promote public awareness of the dangers of desertification.

The GVD is home to some of the longest and largest red sand dunes on Earth.

Atomic Tests at Maralinga and Emu

The British and Australian governments began testing nuclear weapons in the Great Victoria Desert beginning in 1953. A permanent test facility was set up at Maralinga from 1955 to 1963. During that time, both governments tested nuclear weapons that contaminated the area. One such test held on September 27, 1956, involved a nuclear bomb code named One Tree. Radioactive fallout from the test was found throughout Australia. In 1967, a cleanup operation was carried out. In the 1980s, Australian and British armed forces and Aboriginal peoples exposed to the nuclear fallout experienced cancers, blindness, and sores. In 1985, a commission investigated and found that radiation still existed at the Maralinga test site. The area was cleaned again from 1996–2000 at a cost of $108 million. Many believe the area is still contaminated.

The Maralinga Rehabilitation Project worked to clean up radioactive contamination from nuclear testing that occurred at Maralinga from 1955–1963.

Desertification

Desertification occurs when fertile lands are turned into desert areas. UN (United Nations) scientists estimate that the GVD will have 5–15 percent less rainfall by the end of this century unless international groups organize to take action against desertification.

Global Warming

Global warming is the increase in Earth's atmospheric and oceanic temperatures due to an increase in the greenhouse effect. It is one of the causes of desertification in the GVD.

United Nations Convention to Combat Desertification

In 1994, the UN developed a **convention** called the UNCCD (United Nations Convention to Combat Desertification). The Convention was adopted by 194 member countries that work toward preventing and reversing desertification throughout Earth's deserts. The World Day to Combat Desertification is an international celebration that takes place on June 17 every year. The UNCCD declared the first-ever World Day to Combat Desertification on June 17, 1995, to promote public awareness about the dangers of desertification.

Clean Up Australia

Clean Up Australia is an organization dedicated to educating people and encouraging them to clean up the environment. Every year, countries around the world participate in the organization's Clean Up the World campaign. In 2006, the International Year of Deserts and Desertification, the campaign's focus was on deserts and the causes and prevention of desertification. The organization also encourages people living in the GVD area to plant vegetation to protect the soil from drying up and being blown away.

NOTABLE QUOTE

"...and they bought our wheat and wool, so we let them test their bombs, In the heartland of Australia where the black-skinned nation roams...Out on the plains of Maralinga, what happened there was a bloody disgrace. Out on the plains of Maralinga, was total disregard for the Black Australian race."

—From Scottish songwriter Alistair Hulett's song "Plains of Maralinga"

COMPARING THE WORLD'S DESERTS

	Continent	Approximate Size	Type of Desert	Annual Precipitation	Natural Resources
Atacama	South America	40,600 square miles (105,154 sq km)	coastal desert	0.04 inches (1 mm)	copper, sodium nitrate, salt, lithium
Gobi	Asia	500,000 square miles (1,294,994 sq km)	cold desert	2–8 inches (5–20 cm)	oil, coal, copper, gold, petroleum, salt
Great Victoria	Australia	161,700 square miles (418,800 sq km)	hot, dry desert	8–10 inches (20–25 cm)	gold, opal, iron ore, copper, coal, oil
Kalahari	Africa	275,000 square miles (712,247 sq km)	semi-arid desert, arid savannah	5–25 inches (13–64 cm)	coal, copper, nickel, and diamonds
Mojave	North America	25,000 square miles (64,750 sq km)	hot, dry desert	2–6 inches (5–15 cm)	copper, gold, solar power
Sahara	Africa	3.5 million square miles (9.1 million sq km)	hot, dry desert	3 inches (8 cm)	coal, oil, natural gas, various minerals

TIMELINE

About 2.5 billion years ago	The Yilgarn Craton forms
About 2 billion years ago	The Gawler Craton forms
About 1 billion years ago	The Musgrave Range forms
About 38,000 B.C.E.	Aborigine peoples migrate to Australia from what is believed to be India (today)
18,000 B.C.E.	Some Aborigine peoples move inland to central desert areas that include the GVD area
1,000 B.C.E.	The dingo is believed to be introduced to Australia from Southeast Asia
1791	Britain begins to colonize Australia
1875	Explorer Ernest Giles crosses the GVD
1893	Gold is discovered in Australia near the western border of the GVD
1903	The Goldfields Water Supply pipeline is completed
1915	Opals are discovered by Willie Hutchison at Coober Pedy
1947	Australian surveyor Len Beadell creates a rocket-testing range at Woomera; He also begins to create a number of highways or roadways that open up the GVD area
1953	Nuclear weapons begin to be tested at Maralinga and Emu in the GVD
1956	Earth's largest uncut piece of opal is discovered at Coober Pedy
1956–1958	The Gunbarrel Highway is created
1962	Aborigines are given the right to vote in federal government elections in Australia
1965	(September 27)—a nuclear bomb code named One Tree is tested in the GVD
1970	The Mamungari Conservation Park (formerly the Unnamed Conservation Park) is founded
1981	The Anangu Pitjantjatjara Yankunytjatjara Land Rights Act of 1981 is passed which grants Aborigine tribes the rights to manage large areas of land in the GVD
1988	Len Beadell is awarded the Order of Australia
1995	The UNCCD declare the first-ever World Day to Combat Desertification on June 17; The event is held annually around the world
1998	The great desert skink, believed to be extinct, is rediscovered by Aborigine peoples to be living in parts of the GVD
2003	British sculptor Antony Gormley opens his exhibition called *Inside Australia* on the GVD salt lake, Lake Ballard

GLOSSARY

aboriginal Describing the native peoples in a specific area

Aborigines The original or native people that have inhabited Australia for over 40,000 years

convention The union of a group of people dedicated to bringing about a common goal

craton A large block of rock that pushed up from the ocean millions of years ago, and around which a continent grows

diurnal A living thing that is most active during daytime hours

domestic Adapted to living around human beings

feral Describing an animal that was once domesticated, then escaped and became wild

immunity The ability to resist diseases

incubate Provides the proper amount of warmth to an egg so that it will reach maturity and hatch

indigenous The original peoples or native inhabitants of an area

iron oxide A chemical compound that occurs when oxygen mixes with iron

marsupial An animal, such as a kangaroo, that carries its young in a pouch

nocturnal A living thing that is most active during nighttime hours

nomadic Describing people with no fixed home, who instead move from place to place

spinifex Several different kinds of Australian grasses that grow in desert areas

FIND OUT MORE

BOOKS

Bartlett, Anne. *The Aboriginal Peoples of Australia* (First Peoples). Lerner Publications, 2001.

Harris, Nathaniel. *Atlas of the World's Deserts.* The Brown Reference Group, 2003.

Hyde, Natalie. *Desert Extremes* (Extreme Nature). Crabtree Publishing Company, 2009.

Kalman, Bobbie. *Spotlight on Australia* (Spotlight on my Country). Crabtree Publishing Company, 2008.

Kalman, Bobbie and Hadley Dyer. *Australian Outback Food Chains* (Food Chains). Crabtree Publishing Company, 2007.

Latham, Donna. *Deserts* (Endangered Biomes). Nomad Press, 2010.

WEBSITES

IFAD Desertification fact sheet
www.ifad.org/pub/factsheet/desert/e.pdf

Journals of Australian explorers:
http://gutenberg.net.au/explorers-journals.html

Indigenous Protected Areas:
www.environment.gov.au/indigenous/ipa/index.html

The Great Victoria Desert:
www.anra.gov.au/topics/rangelands/overview/sa/ibra-gvd.html

INDEX